Colour Me Father

An Open Letter To My Son

By Paolo Hewitt

THANK YOU – TRULY.

AS DOES RAFI.

Martin Baker, Editor

Lewis Griffiths, Publisher

Simon, Anat, Jo Jo, Ira and Lev Halfon

Johnny, Inki, Stirling and Asa Chandler

Pete, Christine, Hayley and Natalie Garland

Eugene Manzi

Izma Arif

Uzma Arif

Matthew Fryer

Kamal Uddin

Dennis and Hasan Dervish

Mark Lewisohn

Anita Epstein

Simon Wells

Peter, Kin Lin, Grace and Talia Cleak

Kathy and Timothy 'The Bookworm' Pring.

Copyright © Paolo Hewitt

Copyright © Griffiths Publishing

Art work © Rafi Supino-Arif

All Rights Reserved – No part of this publication may be reproduced in any form or by any means without the written permission of the publisher.

ISBN - 9780995653375

For many years, Lord, I would walk down the street and think, 'Just give me one million pounds and all my troubles will be over. Just one million. Please Lord.'

And you refused me. Point blank.

Instead you gave me Rafi, a treasure beyond any riches anywhere in this world.

I can't thank you enough.

Dear Rafi,

I would very much like to talk to you about a smile – a smile that is so deep and so beautiful, it lights up my very soul to even think about it.

The smile of which I write, the smile that impacted so beautifully upon me, crossed your face on August 21st 2016, at around three o' clock in the afternoon.

We were at your first ever birthday party when it happened and not only did you have no inkling at all about what that smile would do to me, it is also fair to say that you had no idea what was actually taking place on that happy day.

All you knew – I think - was that your home was fuller than usual. No doubt, you noted how people, with faces familiar in some small part to you, kept coming up the stairs, bright happiness in their eyes, joy in their words. That's because they had come to celebrate you.

They had come to gather round you and make a fuss of your full being. It is why you believe this world to be so utterly wonderful. Everywhere you go people pick you up and grin and tell you how gorgeous you are, how good-looking, how cute, how beautiful.

Who would not deeply love such a wondrous and loving place where such delight occurs on a daily basis?

On this day, brightly coloured balloons had been placed on the stairs and there was coloured bunting on the bookshelves. Monkeys and elephants smiled and waved to you. You waved back.

Other clues were also present to tip you off that today was out of the norm.

Maybe you noted the amount of food on the table brought to us by your aunties and uncles and friends from the south. Maybe the heightened noise levels caught your attention.

Maybe you had your eye on your presents that existed in bags and parcels out in the hallway.

And maybe you had an idea, when we departed for the park later that day and slid down slides, pushed swings and watched the little ones run and run, that something special was taking place.

Maybe. Maybe. Maybe.

I do know this, though.

When your birthday cake was carried into the room it gave me a memory, an image, I will never forget. For it gave me the smile. Correction. *You* gave me the smile.

This is what happened.

Your cake, carrying a single candle was brought in from the kitchen and placed on the table in front of you.

When the candle was lit, you were in your mother's arms. You stared at the candle light. You were beautifully beguiled by that candle light. It mesmerised you.

And then it happened. Everyone sang you Happy Birthday. And then they *applauded*. You had your back to everyone but as soon as the applause began you turned and that is when you gave them the smile, the most beautiful smile, a smile that seemed to be say - *this is for me, all for me? Thank you so much.*

But - most importantly - your smile also said in no ambivalent or ambiguous way - *isn't life just wonderful?* And in doing so you taught me a valuable truth.

I am now going to talk to you about pigeons. You love them. Every time we are out, and you spot one, your arm shoots out. *There! There!* Your favourite pigeon spot is the small park at the end of our street. For me, this park sums up London.

At times, early in the morning, as the sun breaks through the trees, like God at your window, it is heart-stirring. Many times, I have stopped the pram so you and I can exult in its beauty.

Even in winter, with the trees robbed of their colour, the sky an oppressive grey, filled in by a blanket of clouds, there is still an austere beauty present in this landscape that I want you to experience.

Yet sins, grave sins, mark and scar this ground. One rape, two stabbings took place here in the last month alone. The beauty and the beast live side by side in this place, Rafi. And that is London.

Your finger shoots out. *There! There!* I push the pram towards a pigeon poking at some food, like a Northern Soul dancer's head on speed. And as we get *this* close to this edgy bird with its jittery movement, it flaps, and flies away. And yet you are not disappointed for you love to watch that bird soar out of view. You love to watch its' flight. It thrills you to watch its' ascension into the sky, onto a tree, maybe a nearby roof, better still a nearby TV aerial.

And so do I. Never did before. But now you are making me see the magic of it all.

Then we see another one and off we go, chasing pigeons but never grasping one.

Raffini, when I saw that smile on your face, I realised that my biggest job in life right now, is both simple and monumental – to keep you believing without a moment's hesitation in your soul, that life is indeed deeply wonderful.

And to do that I must make sure your dreams never act like those pigeons.

For some of mine have Rafi and I know the hurt that brings.

After Mass the other day, I spoke with Sister Patricia. She always asks me how you are. 'How is the heir apparent and King to the throne?' she asks in that lovely lively manner of hers.

'He is so well,' I tell her.

And then I show her pictures of you and I am always so quietly moved when I see how happy you look and act in these pictures.

My swallowing of emotion is not at all surprising. I am so quick to tears since you arrived on this earth.

Just by existing, you have opened me up emotionally. The smallest events serve to cut me the deep.

Television. The lovely Mary tells Norris she has a baby son that she gave away at 14 years of age and my tears gather. Warm Robert marries Amy and there I go again – turning my face away from you, desperately shielding my upset, so anxious not to cause you any unnecessary disturbance.

Fictional stories, fictional characters, real people – does not matter. Still my tears fall. A trailer for a programme about scientists who have dedicated so much to helping the physically impaired – yep you got it. There I go again, swallowing hard.

Sometimes it is not the television or the record or a piece of art that is invading me and triggering me so. Sometimes, Rafi, it is just you.

For there are times I just sit and watch you playing with your toys, so beautifully unencumbered by awareness, and as I gaze at your attention, fully mastered by some toy or other, I feel so moved. In the absolute depths of my soul I feel such strong yearnings and they are all directed towards securing your very happiness.

Or maybe you are staring out of the window, your deep brown eyes wondering and a'wondering, and I look at you and the next thing I know I am choked from unexpected sorrowing.

This scene occurs many times, Rafi, and I have no idea why I am weeping so.

Normally, on such occasions, I know where to go for the answer - my pulverised childhood, that terrible time I experienced as a small child, when a woman visited upon me such cruelty that deep suffering and unimaginable pain became constant friends of mine for far too many years.

Yet I cannot find the reason for my crying there.

Many times in the past, when gloom has enveloped me, it is precisely those deep wounds that are at the centre of my sadness. But not now, for these tears I cry are not related to that time of agony and harmful deep laceration to my spirit

I turn my attention away from the past and think of the present - but that too yields nothing. In fact, right now I feel blessed Rafi. You are here and so is love. How could I not feel its beautiful force?

And so I go inward again and I think of the future - but nothing there either. The fact of the matter is that no matter how hard I search I can find no reason for my tears.

And then this thought occurs.

Maybe, just maybe, it is because you have done what no one else thought could be done and you put the joy inside my fears and that these tears that surge into my eyes are nothing more than the tears of immeasurable gratitude for your presence on this earth, an acknowledgement that just your breath alone signals to my soul that the very real possibility of a healing of my deep hurt has finally arrived.

Not that I tell you of these tears in any way to engage your sympathy. I *like* crying, Rafi. I *like* letting it all out, I *like* the stormless sensation, the warmth afterwards, spreading up and down my body. After crying, I feel ready for life again. I feel strong, purified, *cleansed.* Maybe you feel the same way.

'You can give him everything you never had as a child,' Sister Patricia tells me. 'What a wonderful thing that is. And remember,' she admonishes, 'be faithful to life.'

What a lovely phrase. Be faithful to life. I have thought about that a lot, and I think she means never throw away what God gives you. And what God gave you – amongst so many things - was that smile.

Right now, however Rafi, you are not smiling. Right now, you are standing in front of the television and you are shouting at it. *Da! Da!*

I look over and the Labour leader Jeremy Corbyn suddenly appears in front of you. I have to beam and grin because you and Jeremy have already met.

You probably won't remember for the simple fact that you were not born at the time. But don't let that small fact worry you.

It happened about 30 hours before your arrival on this earth. I don't know if you can stretch your memory back that far but it was a Thursday. Your mother, Uncle Im, and myself, had been living at the Whittington Hospital for two days.

During that time a doctor had advised your mother to do as much walking as possible. This made sense. I don't know if you recall but we went to that small garden outside the hospital, where there are benches and small gracious plants and flowers, and we sat for a while under an unsummery sky and I remember I was glad for the cool air: great heat would not have been of aid to your mother.

We talked a little, and then we stood and turned and went back inside again. By this time your mother was moving slow, real slow, and feeling very tired. You were sucking up all her energy.

When we came back inside she asked to sit on some chairs placed against a wall before tackling the escalators.

As we watched the hospital flow go by I suddenly spotted a bearded, slim man coming down the escalators. The instinct towards recognition hit me inside.

I nudged your mother. 'Is that...?'

'Yes it is. I recognise him from school.'

Your mother's school is in Jeremy Corbyn's constituency. He often visits.

In for a penny, in for a - 'Jeremy!' I shouted. He stopped. Looked over. He was totally alone. No entourage. No PAs. No secretaries. Just Jeremy. On his own.

I stood up and went straight to him. I put out my hand. 'I have to shake your hand for what you are doing,' I told him. And he took my hand and he smiled.

I should explain something here Rafi. The Labour party had been set up to protect and further the interests of the working class but, of late it had abandoned those roots. Corbyn had been elected by exasperated men and women who wanted to pull Labour back to its left wing roots. I was one of those - hence my delight in the man.

At that particular time......

But I am not here to talk politics. Far from it. All you should know was that as soon as he became Leader of the party, sections of the UK media, arrogant in their power, savaged the man relentlessly. The attacks were vicious, horrible to see. They tore at his name, tore apart his character, tore into his beliefs. They are still doing it.

But he stood firm, Rafi, would not budge. And that is an important lesson in life. No matter what the world around you is saying, no matter what those close say, no matter what *I am* saying, if it feels right inside, if you know with certainty it is a correct way to go, then take that road for that is your heart guiding you and the heart is always true. Always.

The head might be more sensible, more cautious, but in life the heart gives you your true destination.

Jeremy had kept to his designs, and to do that required a confidence that for a long time I deeply coveted.

On the surface I should never have been the keeper of jealousy when it came to strong self-possession in others. After all, I had achieved what I had set out to do in life – I was a 'success.' I had achieved my ambition. I had become a writer. Against all the odds.

How did that happen? Simple.

When I was fourteen years old I walked into school and came across Enzo Esposito in the common room, a man whose blood, like some of mine, is derived from the Neapolitan area of Italy; this has always made us truly *simpatico* to each other.

He was sat at a table absorbed in a newspaper. I rarely saw him like this. Most of my closest links at that time were not readers. English literature classes at my school had seen them off. At age 13, we had suddenly switched – no warning given – from the delight of Dickens to the language of Chaucer and Shakespeare. These stories were told in an alien language. Unprepared for such demands, many of my friends lost all interest in books.

It was cruel and misguided. One of the richest worlds built by man shut off to them in a moment by the very system set up to enlighten them. As a friend of mine often cries when exasperated with the world, it makes no sense!

I only survived because I could not live without the safety books had offered me since I was six years old. I had to believe there had to be something in these incomprehensible passages that would prove to be of value to me.

My friends had no such requirements.

They were too sharp, too ahead. I remember when the record by Rupie Edwards called Irie Feelings (Skanga) came on the radio for the very first time. I had never heard such a disjointed record, wondered how anybody could even like such scatter brained music.

They on the other hand got it straight away. They went to clubs and danced to it time and time again.

They always were a year ahead of me.

I asked Enzo what the publication in his hand was. He told me it was a music paper. I had never heard of such a thing. At that time, the most important things in the world to me were records, books and football. And gaining the love of Teresa Driver. I knew of nothing else - certainly not publications that focused solely on music,

After further questioning, he handed over the paper. I saw it was called the NME. I sat down and opened it and within a minute the light had gone on, and my life's ambition had been made absolutely clear. How lucky was I Rafi? To know at such an early age that this is what I wanted to be, that this was where I had to go.

I have known so many people so much smarter and brighter than me who have walked around in circles for year after year, never knowing what to do until life finally threw up its arms in exasperation and settled them. Nature after all abhors a vacuum.

I had no such experience. I had been blessed with a road to follow. *O lucky boy*, you could say of me. Over the next few weeks I became obsessed with the NME. Over the next few months I fixated on becoming a music writer.

In August 1973, I went to see my favourite band, The Faces, at the Reading Festival. The music paper Sounds had a tent there. I marched in and told them I wanted to write for them. I didn't. I wanted to write for the NME. But I figured I had to start somewhere.

The man in front of me told me I was in the wrong place and to go to the offices in London. He looked at me curiously. I think he saw the obsession in my eyes. In fact, he must have done so because that obsession was vital and very present in me.

In my special town, I only knew of one other guy who shared my ambition. I went to college with him but I knew he would not make it. Why? Because this was not a matter of life and death for him - and it was for me.

That obsession not only pushed me onwards, but it had other purposes, other vital attributes. It allowed me to absorb some terrible blows and yet still carry on my quest.

One day, I let down my guard. I told my English teacher of my burning desire. I told her I wanted to be a writer. A music writer. She was a spinster, a woman whose life revolved around literature. I thought she would understand. I thought she would advise me. I thought she and I could work together to realise this idea.

But she didn't.

Instead, she laughed. Right into my face.

Instantly, I was hurled backwards to the humiliation and fear that had coloured my childhood so heavily, and instantly I did what I did as a child – I closed my mouth, bowed my head and endured the terrible sound of rejection.

Then I got away from her as quickly as I could.

Later on, as I lay miserable in bed, a sense of fear took me. I could not help thinking that if my life plan only engendered amusement from the adult world, then what terrible fate awaited me?

If I could not be what I yearned to be then what was my destination? I knew I had a path to follow but at that point I had no idea where the path was actually located. How did one even become a music writer? I had no idea how to begin the journey let alone successfully finish it.

And if the search for the path was already being viewed by some as ridiculous then surely I was wrong headed to even entertain such thoughts.

Yet I had no alternatives. I knew that my soul would never be sated or satisfied unless I had truly attempted to achieve that which I desired above all.

But that is the great thing about obsession. It cannot help itself. Whatever is thrown at it is always rebuffs. It can't be hurt, can't be beaten down, or extinguished. It can only grow. If it is right, it can only flourish. It has no other way of being.

Obsession took the sound of my English teacher's laughter and deleted it. It would not take acidic criticism. It said, *forget her, what does she know of such things?*

And then it pushed me forward, all the while shielding me from the blows to come.

I met musicians at gigs and asked for interviews. They turned me down. My obsession said, *Sod you, one day you will be knocking on my door.*

And they did.

I wrote letters to the music papers that were never acknowledged. *No worries, they will call one day.*

And they did.

My obsession now showed me quite forcibly that I would have to leave my Surrey town if I was to realise that which consumed me day and night. My obsession gave me the keys to do so. It sat me down and gave me a plan.

At age 21 I landed in London and went to college. The first thing I did when I got there was to sign up to write for the student paper, a publication named Fuse.

Fuse allowed me to interview bands that played the college and review records.

One week I wrote about Rod Stewart. A girl in the same hall that I lived in wrote a stinging rebuke of my words in a letter and put it under my door and demanded we talk. I went to her room and we were kissing an hour later.

As our lips entwined I opened my eyes and my obsession winked at me. And then discreetly left me to it.

But what truly brought me happiness, Rafi, was the discovery, the marvellous discovery, that in London, you could buy the NME from Camden tube station on Tuesday lunchtime. In my Surrey town, I had to wait until Thursday afternoon.

Now everything was Tuesday. At about 12 I would leave college and rush to the newsstand opposite the ticket barrier and buy the NME. I would then rush back, find a quiet corner and study it, and study it hard.

By now, I was fixated on the writers. I knew their musical preferences, their writing styles and their faces. I looked at pictures of them and imagined myself in their place. I thought them so glamorous. I thought if only I can do that, stand around in cool clothes talking about bands, people clicking their fingers at me and saying, *'Great article man,'* and then my life would be wondrous and my soul cleansed of all fear and doubt and anxiety. I thought if I became a NME writer I could truly say I had a family, all of us writers so hip and cool, bonded together by a deep love for music and literature.

This is the paradise I yearned for from deep inside my soul every minute of the day.

At gigs I would study the crowd to see if any writers were present. If they were I would slide up next to them and nod at them. If they nodded back I was both stricken with shyness and ecstatic at their recognition of my presence.

And then one day I arrived at Camden tube and the newsagent blithely, offhandedly, *casually* informed me that the NME had sold out for that week. There were no copies available. At all.

I did not believe him. No way, Signor. Im-*possible*.

I stood there for five minutes and I argued with him.

'Aren't there any out back?'

'No, sold out mate.'

'You haven't got one left?'

'No. Told you. Sold out.'

'There's not one spare copy you might have dropped...'

A stare of great exasperation mixed with anger is trained upon me.

'Not one......'

In the end I bought Melody Maker. MM was NME's rival. I figured if I could not get the heroin, I would have to settle for the methadone. That was because for many of us, Melody Maker was deeply unhip, a relic, a paper held down by its' readers' reverence for bands which in that period of time, no interest could be shown for one second. I speak of the likes of Led Zeppelin, Genesis, and the Rolling Stones.

Truth was, in the early 70s I had had serious relationships with all of them. I had gone to their gigs (Genesis at Reading Festival 1973, Led Zep and The Stones at Earls Court) and bought their albums. I had read all their interviews and in some cases acquired books about them.

But of course, fickle in teenage, when the NME crowed three times and deemed them out of favour, I turned my back on them.

Melody Maker, on the other hand, had remained faithful.

I got to college, disappointed, annoyed. I flicked open Melody Maker with a deep sigh - and suddenly became very interested. For there before me an advert – Young Writers Wanted.

I paused. Thought. I got out my copies of Fuse and found some scissors. I carefully extracted my work. I placed about five articles bearing my name in an envelope and wrote a covering letter. I posted the letter and went home and thought, *'Of this nothing will come.'*

On Thursday, a phone call. Would I come to the Melody Maker office Friday night and meet the paper's editor, Richard Williams?

Yes I would.

On that Friday night, Rafi, when I walked into Richards's office the first thing I saw was that Richard had hung on his wall a huge picture of the 1970 Italian team.

'Do you like football?' I asked.

Within a year I had left college and was a staff member on the paper.

Whenever I think of this major event in my life I am always bothered by one question: if the NME *had* been available for sale that day in Camden I would never have seen the MM advert so how would my life have been different? What sequence of events would have then taken place? Had I been guided? Or had my obsession been so great that my later life as a music writer was inevitable?

I now think the latter, that my obsession placed me every Tuesday at Camden Tube station. In other words, I was in position, ready for the opportunity my longing yearned for every night.

Because of this, the world bent to my imaginings and then delivered them. I met major musicians. I spoke with Marvin Gaye and did so at too young an age. I did not know my music then, did not know jazz, blues, doo-wop, all of which had helped shape his own work. I wish I could interview him now. I would have him pinned down for four days.

I talked with Stevie Wonder and half-way through the interview - which took place in a dressing room in France with about 30 people watching - I suddenly had a paralysing thought - *I am sitting one yard away from Stevie Wonder, Stevie Wonder that is, one of the very few people I consider a genius.*

In an instant the words from my heart got stuck in my throat.

Stevie kept saying, 'Any more questions?' and all I could reply was, 'Yeah…just a minute…yeah you remember that song…yeah….'

I met Bruce Springsteen and in doing so I learnt how the private could impinge on the public in ruinous ways.

It was a bitter lesson, Rafi, and one I still regret.

In 1980 I had hailed Springsteen's The River album in a highly laudatory review. Because of my words, I got to meet the man and interview him. I liked him. A lot. He was soulful and sincere and we got on well. After playing for nearly four hours, he then invited me into his dressing room and gave me all the time I needed. He could not have been more helpful.

In fact, he sought me out after one show to apologise for not being able to talk further.

A year later he released an acoustic album named Nebraska. And it was brilliant. People still talk about it now. Just Bruce and an acoustic guitar and simple but foreboding songs.

I was asked to review it by a senior editor who, as he handed the album to me, made very clear his utter dislike of Springsteen. I took serious note of his leanings.

I went home and instead of lauding this brave work I played to the senior editor's prejudices - and castigated the album. I pulled it apart. Song-by-song. And why? Because I was people-pleasing, Rafi, looking to be liked by this man, looking to avoid confrontation. I was not strong enough in myself to stand my ground.

I should have completely ignored this man and told the world what a brave and wonderful album this was – but I didn't. I caved in. I was weak.

I played to another man's tastes. Adopted them as my own. Bad move. People-pleasing only leads into bad waters, Rafi, because it creates a great dishonesty within you, forces you to wear a mask. You give yourself away to fit in with another and the price for that is far too high.

So to Bruce Springsteen - *Sono molto dispiaciuto per mio comportamento.* I really am.

In this time of which I speak, I travelled the world. For nothing. Money from record companies took me to Japan and Australia and America and nearly all of Europe.

I attended gig after gig for nothing. I was handed free records. I was given free lunches. I entered prestigious clubs for nothing. People nodded at me. I had a small kind of fame by my side, although that particular illusion was never part of my *modus operandi*. I was seen as a man of importance.

And then it happened to me, the dream was made real. I stood in an office with other writers and a fellow writer walked in, clicked his fingers and said, 'Hey nice article this week Paolo.'

Given that situation, most people would have been exhilarated at their dream's realisation. A spring in their step would suddenly be fashioned. A strong and healthy joy would be placed in their heart. It would direct them towards such fruitful experiences.

And yet, I felt absolutely nothing of the sort.

In fact, I felt the opposite - deeply anxious and gravely insecure. On top of that, I habitually, on a daily basis, remained absolutely scathing about my work, my talent and my abilities. The 'Hey nice article' medicine for all my ills had failed to take. In fact, I got sicker.

At one point in this deeply torturous time, I truly and utterly believed that I had been given my dream job out of pity. I thought that IPC, the publishers of Melody Maker, owned a computer in which they had inserted my name and the message they got back was that I had been raised from the age of ten in a children's home - so let's be nice to the orphan. *He's a crap writer but let's show some pity here guys. Bit of charity never went amiss.*

Truly I thought that, Rafi, and that miserable thought haunted me every day, in my life and in my dreams - and I could not shake it - and I never want you to feel like that. Ever.

I believed I was absolutely talentless. I did. Even when the world patted me on the back I would not be persuaded otherwise.

People would say to me *nice piece you wrote last week,* and I would nod, but all the time be thinking: *you're so far off it's embarrassing, it was crap, it was awful, didn't you see how the opening line had been ripped off from some NME writer, Julie Burchill or Tony Parsons, occasionally Ian McDonald and Nick Kent. And could you not see how bad my description of their music was, how pedantic some of my passages were*?

And yet there I was saying thanks and smiling.

The truth is I wanted everything I wrote to be perfect. Perfect, perfect, perfect. So I devised rules. Never start an article with a quote, or the words 'And' or 'The.' Always come up with a great and original opening line.

And if I broke those rules, I would be depressed for days. I really would. I'd torment myself. *You are useless. You started that article with a quote. Pathetic. What did you say? Never open with a quote. Now look at you .You can't even abide by your own rules. Weak. Weak. Weak.*

Every day, I harmed my very soul in such a manner.

But then, salvation. One morning, it was early and I noticed that suddenly the world looked and felt clear and clean. I was standing in the kitchen of my north-London home gazing out at London, and then my heart intervened. It spoke to me.

It told me - *this path you have taken will not be easy to traverse. There are obstacles in your way not least yourself. But you will succeed. Keep going. Don't give up. You will succeed. You will succeed. You will succeed.*

And that was my heart and my heart was true for that was the spirit inside all of us speaking. So I followed His words. I collected myself up and dismissed all thoughts of quitting. I pushed forward. Took a lot of blows along the way. People can be very nasty. And malicious. And envious. But they can also be encouraging and funny and beautiful and they made me smile and they pushed me on and I am forever grateful for their protection.

One big problem I had was my shyness. Which was so often mistaken for arrogance. I nodded when they expected words. I stayed silent when they looked for my opinion. I did not conform to their idea of a music writer. They felt that I was ignoring them. That I was too much of a 'name' to bother with them. Truth was I feared them so I kept them at bay.

And now I stand before you and I do so carrying a conviction that I feel incumbent to pass to you Rafi. Do with it what you will.

In this life, if you are lucky enough to be driven to achieve an idea of yourself, driven by a dream, it will materialise. It is true. Ask and it will be given. Knock long enough and eventually the door opens. James Brown the great musician knew about this. He once called an album of his, Mind Power. That is what I am referring to.

You remember my friend, Russell? We had coffee with him the other morning? That's the one.

Well, I met him at the same time as the events just described. Very close friend, he soon became. Russell too had the obsession on him.

But his was not for music, it was for money. He spoke of it constantly. How to earn it. How to keep it. How to work it.

In fact, one day I had to tell him to shut up talking about it. He was money, money, money. And I was music, music, music. (Although that does do Russ a disservice – he too was music and very discerning and sharp about it. The man had Nick Drake on his turntable a good ten years before I even began to understand the beauty in that man's work.)

What happened to Russ? Do you have to ask? He ended up in a lovely part of the world with a swimming pool and a tennis court in his backyard. His thinking, his mind - brought him there.

'Imagination is everything,' Albert Einstein said, and then added, 'It is the preview of life's coming attractions.'

Russ imagined the house and the pool and tennis court and he did so for many waking hours. I imagined the music writer's life. And both of us realised the film we ran in our minds.

I also see that luck was by my side. I was from care. That meant I did not have shackles placed upon me. I did not have parents demanding I stay in my Surrey town and play it safe. I did not have a dominant father insisting I go into the family business. Care freed me up and gave me the freedom to achieve.

It allowed me to go to London with no baggage. Care is perfect for artists. It is why Bob Dylan really wanted to be an orphan. Orphans roam free. Orphans have great courage. Orphans are bestowed with romanticism.

As the motto of my football club says Rafi - To Dare Is To Do - which brings us back Jeremy.

'But Jeremy,' I said, 'much as I love what you have been doing, you have one policy all wrong.'

His face turned quizzical. 'What policy?'

'You support Arsenal,' I replied.

He smiled, knowingly. 'Spurs, I take it.'

Then he asked what I was doing in the hospital. I pointed to your mother and said, 'We are waiting on our baby. His mother actually knows you from her work.'

'Really?' he replied. 'Well let's meet her.' And he came over and they spoke and then Jeremy asked how long we had been waiting for you to arrive. *Two days,* we told him.

'Right,' he said, completely unexpectedly, 'let's start up a song.'

And, there on the spot, he began chanting, 'Come on baby come on - come on baby come on.' And we joined in. 'Come on baby come on,' and it was good, Rafi, a real good moment. Never forget it.

Then he had to go, and when I nodded to him - and I won't forget this either - he hit his heart with his hand and walked off. At that moment, in 2015, I thought him noble and dignified and strong.

And I thought, *I so hope you become a Prime Minister* because then I could sit you down one day and tell you, Rafi, my darling young son, the second person to ever sing to you was the Prime Minister of this country.

Who was the first person? Why me, of course. And that song was *Twinkle, Twinkle, Little Star.*

Your mother and I had been told that we should sing a particular song to you every night whilst you lay in her stomach, and that when you appeared and we sang that song to you again, there would be instant recognition on your part and thus we would be bonded ever deeper.

I chose *Twinkle, Twinkle, Little Star*. I love its melody and imagery. It conjures up a world at peace with itself, a peace I have yearned for myself on so many occasions.

Every night, I would gently whisper that song into your mother's stomach, more spoken than sung (for I am tone deaf), wondering whom I was singing to.

I then imagined you as a toddler, hearing that song and then smiling at me in deep recognition. But it is yet to happen.

I have sung it to you a thousand times. You could not care less. Even now, at the stay and play events I take you to, when they sing the song, I always look to you to see if there is any recognition in our face. There never is. You just stand there, unblinking. Like I said, yet to happen.

And in thinking about that song, it amuses me now how the songs of your baby years have now taken centre place in my mind.

Before, I used to walk down the street with Al Green in my head, or The Isley Brothers, or The Staple Singers or Bobby Parris or Freddy Scott, and so many others it was ridiculous. Now it is *Zoom Zoom We Are Going To The Moon* or *The Monkey Song* that invades my head. I rid myself of this music as quickly as possible, and lie back and think of Motown, but no good, another one of your songs quickly pops back. *Wind the bobbin up, wind the bobbin up, pull, pull....*

I do note one song with great interest, which is *Row The Boat* whose opening verse runs, *Row row, row the boat gently down the stream, merrily, merrily, merrily, merrily – life is but a dream.*

How cool a concept is that is to be singing to the young? One worthy of many volumes, of many discussions, I would say. And if that song is right then maybe our purpose is clear - to wake up.

I think that is what has defined my latter years - waking up to potential, to possibilities, to hearing the songs of experience and, most importantly, ridding myself of illusions.

Illusions are a big obstacle in life, Rafi – a big problem. I have fallen for them time and time again. Kiss Teresa Driver and all will be well. It wasn't. (Nice way to find out though.)

Get a staff job at the NME and all your problems will disappear. Did not happen. Life got worse, in fact.

Make ten million pounds and live in magic for the rest of your life. Still to try that one out.

Illusions are what we are sold every minute of every day. They reside in adverts, billboards, newspaper articles and a million other different places. Do this, do that, get this, get that and then all will be well. But it won't be. It's a con.

The only way to the happiness they promise you – as far as I am concerned - is to go inside yourself. If your inside is healthy then it is advantage you all of your life. I promise you that.

Oscar said it in De Profundis. 'The spirit alone is of importance.' Marcus Aurelius told the Romans and the world yet to come, 'You have power over your mind - not outside events.'

James Allen was there too – 'The turmoil of the world we cannot avoid, but the disturbances of the mind we can overcome.'

On the day that I write these words, December $4^{t,}$ 2016, there is great anxiety afoot. The Americans have made Donald Trump their president. He is a loose cannon, a belligerent, highly insecure man whose mission to make America 'great' lies in an assertion of strength which twists itself into the defining mood of these times – that of bullying.

Bullying is everywhere. It has replaced discussion, debate. You stand against me? You disagree? Then I will attack you and demean you and seek to humiliate you. I will not engage in two way communication. I will assert my position as the correct one and then bully down your beliefs.

On June 23rd 2016 Britain voted to leave the European Union. People who were against such a move, who are deeply worried by its implications, are told to simply shut up. *You lost, we won. Now on your bike.*

Many worry that the effect on the British economy will be tragic. They are dismissed out of hand as 'gloomy' prophets. Others detect a rise in bellicose nationalism. Those visibly not of English stock have been insulted and attacked since the vote.

It adds to the growing sense of chaos and instability, the deep worry experienced by many,

In the Middle East, solutions to terrible wars, seem out of reach. Western cities remain under constant threat from terror attacks. In the UK it is estimated a quarter of a million people will tonight have no home to shelter them from the cold and the storms.

I read this the other day: 'We have tried our hand at the architecture of world peace, and have failed. We are in the grip of economic forces which we can no longer control. The social structures we have built are crumbling. It is the hour of disillusion and helplessness and growing fear.'

Which kind of sums up the general feeling.

Except that last passage was written in 1937. In the 1980s I was aghast that America was led by Ronald Reagan, Britain by Margaret Thatcher and the opposition was led by Michael Foot, a left winger whose radical views and character were eviscerated daily by the media.

Forty years later, I am aghast that America is led by Donald Trump, Britain by Theresa May and the opposition is led by Jeremy Corbyn, a left winger whose radical views…. You get my drift.

I do not for one millisecond make light of the problems facing the world, for they are vast, with potential to create enormous harm and I worry about the world you will have to inhabit, but I do make the point that every decade, every generation, has felt the same way about their world and yet somehow, it keeps on turning, keeps going, that one day it's kicks and the next day it's kicks in the shins.

Fear and terror and anxiety feed into people but even so, here comes the summer, the autumn, the winter and the spring, and every day come new arrivals such as yourself, Rafi, to help shape the world into a better place, to breathe positive life and energy into it, and hopefully – with what little we can give you - to do your very best, for it, to live well, to above all to treat others as you would be treated yourself.

Short of an assassination attempt, I can do nothing about Donald Trump becoming President. Nothing at all. But I can stage a revolution, and that revolution is a revolution of my mind. For, like Oscar, I have grown tired *'of the articulate utterances of men.'*

Read The Bible. Read Aurelius and Fox and Tolle. Read a million others. And then see the world your way and not theirs.

For me, magic is all around. I look up and see the clouds carrying the secrets of the world to unknown destinations. Leaves are words left on the ground for me to read and absorb. Trees are explosions of delight that then delight by leaning into grandeur. Oceans breathe and rivers chatter, chatter, chatter. Aeroplanes are merely sharks that fly.

Einstein again. 'Strive not to be a success but to be of value.'

Or perhaps not. Maybe you will find happiness in that which holds no meaning for me. I play football. You play rugby. I think spiritual. You think materially.

Perhaps you will own a house on Bishops Avenue and its size and grandeur will bring you deep joy. Money may drive you in the way it drove Russ. You may own banks. All over the world.

But if you do, be careful. Addiction dwells in money. History counts many brought to their knees by their insistent and monstrous desire for cash, deep wounds inflicted by the lengths they will go to for its acquisition.

Beware the greed money induces, Rafi. Avoid it at all costs, for it will determine and dominate your life to the exclusion of all, including love, freedom and family.

And beware fame as well. The majority think it the pinnacle of life. the ultimate achievement. They see it as a panacea for all their problems. I think them wrong.

For sure, a tiny percentage of people are suited to its demands, its weird rhythms and nature. They wear it well and maybe you will as well.

But as far as I can see, for many, fame just brings misery. People think it has magical powers, but it doesn't and it can't and it won't and it will never cure the hurt inside. In fact, I think it just adds to it.

Or maybe such advice is not at all required and you will eschew the world, down all tools and go and work and live with the poor.

Does not matter to me. Not important. As long as you glow on the inside, that is of the greatest importance to me, Rafi, and that is what I strive to give you in my own small way.

Why? Because a man who is in harmony with himself is a man who is in harmony with the world. (Bit more Aurelius for you there, Rafi. I would try and think of something new and totally original to give you, but as the Bible states - nothing new under the sun.)

You can give nothing better to this world than the beauty of your soul and thus add to the sum of the world's happiness. And it will be difficult to do so. People will come to you and they will resent you your happiness, simply because they are so deeply unhappy themselves.

They are battered and bruised and because of that they will insult you and trick you, and manipulate you and throw punches and break your heart and disappoint you and cause you to cry tears that you never knew were so bitter, and their actions will suggest to you that a life of the spirit is of no value.

And maybe they have a point. Maybe this world *is* a Godless and a cruel arena. Maybe we are born, we live, we die and there is nothing else beyond this point. Perhaps my inner journey is a waste of time. And risible. That is not the point. I just want you to be aware of all possibilities, all roads and to take the one which speaks to you the deepest without any fear at all of its consequences.

I also believe that the life of the spirit is far more *interesting*, endures longer, and offers much more than other illusions and temptations.

It is an adventure which never ceases, which offers up new insights each day. I hope you take the road less offered by society. I want you to know all that life has to offer.

I have no doubt you will.

I started to think this way some twenty five years or so before your arrival.

How did that happen? Simple.

I was tired of the harsh voices in my head that screamed at my soul that I have just written about. They dominated my life. I could experience joy but it was always – *always* - tempered by a wicked voice inside of me that spoke of how undeserving I was to receive such gifts. It was as if every time the sun shone on me a cloud quickly appeared to block out the sunlight.

In my twenties I gave into this voice, feebly acquiesced to its diagnosis. I was weak, ineffectual, talentless.

And in believing this I truly felt that happiness would never be mine to master or to experience.

As the years passed, the weight of that message slowly crushed me. By the time I reached my early thirties it had worn me out. I was tired, I was tired of being sad. Tired of being tired of it.

In your early thirties – thankfully - wisdom starts to gather inside. You start to understand the world and your place in it a little better, and therefore you start to imagine a new way forward.

You want to move upwards now. You want and need change.

I did, anyway and so in that spirit, something led me to buy a book, called How To Heal Yourself.

This contained an idea that spun me around completely. The author, Louise L. Hay posited the following – if you are going to spend your time viciously attacking yourself inside, why not reverse the process? There are no odds here.

You've tried bad and look where that has taken you. Why not travel the other way? Think well about yourself. See what that brings

That idea, that simple little idea, was massive for me. I put it to the test. It hit me hard and it exhilarated me. I put it to the test again. I rejected the voices inside and replaced them. You are a good writer, Paolo, you are a good writer. You have talent.

It was like a blast of deep light scattering the darkness. A feeling of extreme well-being rose up inside of me. Result? A dissolving of bad started to happen inside of me, an opening up to warmth and kindness and generosity. I liked the feeling.

I searched for more books, looking to go deeper and deeper. And in doing so discovered a man by the name of Emmet Fox whose words and ideas rang so true to me - and that led me back to God. Or Spirit. Or Higher Being.

Funny, how hesitated using the G word there for fear of – what? Ridicule by others? Cruel laughter on the winds directed at me? Why should that be so? After all, God is real and true to billions of people on this earth. Every day and every night, countless people drop to their knees and offer up their sincere prayers of gratitude. Why should I be any different?

It is a knee jerk reaction, one forged in my past when I ran so scared of people's opinions of me, and sought to please as many people as possible. Now I make my stand which forever shall be.

Faith is ridiculed in this country and perhaps that has made me think of previous friends who would rubbish my convictions.

For they all knew other versions of me. Some were acquainted with a man of cynicism and narrow mindedness. Others knew a man determined to take for pleasure at all costs. Still more knew a man who railed at God for his luck in life. But the men that once went under my name have long since passed on. Hallelujah.

My next project may well be a biography of the great songwriter, Ronnie Lane. He once asked of his musical friend, Charlie Hart, 'Charlie, a do gooder is someone who just does good, right?' And Charlie replied, 'That's right Ronnie.'

And then Lane replied, 'then why do people use it as a put down? If you do good how can it be bad?' Good question Ronnie. And then Charlie sunk his head in his hands for that morning he had a hangover the size of London. Courtesy of Ronnie who had obviously done him....badly.

People will talk to you about freedom, Rafi, but they only want you to have the freedom to be what *they* want you to be, (usually a carbon copy of themselves,)not what your heart demands you be. There is a big gulf between the two.

All I know is that I believe for certain that you are a gift from God, sent here for many purposes not least that of healing your father.

That notion is as true to me as water and air are sweet.

I thought of God many times just before you were born, Rafi, a time when - and I can't believe this now - you were a complete abstraction to me.

Impossible for me to now imagine, but that is exactly what you were at this point in my life – you my darling young son, were invisible.

Your mother told me she was with you in December of 2015, and once the shock of happiness and wonderment and fear had subsided, I just could not see or imagine you in any way whatsoever. To think of you as real was beyond me. I stayed that way for many months. I just could not imagine – you.

In that time, everything revolved around your mother. How was she? Was everything okay? How did she feel? Sick? Anxious?

(And by the way, Rafi, at some point in life you may come across a theory that before they are born children actually choose their parents. They look around and decide *okay, those two*. If this is true, then congratulations - you made the best choice for a mother. Really, you could not have chosen better. Really. Cherish her, man, for she is exceptional.)

Even when we went to see midwives and doctors, and sat in small rooms where they hooked your mother to a machine and your heartbeat was played to us, and so loud and insistent was that sound it reminded me of raves I had attended - still you were not real.

Your heartbeat then was like receiving a message from outer space.

Then, one day, as the big day approached, your auntie kindly gave us some clothes. One night, I unpacked them, laid them out on the bed, and then looked down upon them.

And then suddenly it hit me. *'Damm, not long from now and all being well, someone is going to be wearing these clothes, an actual living being that I am responsible for.'* And I gasped and I sat down and I caught my breath - and that was when you placed yourself right at the centre of my consciousness.

What would this person look like? We knew you were a boy, but what kind of boy? What kind of baby? What kind of human being? Would you even *like* me? (Those voices again...) And that is when you became real, very, very real.

The day after we met Jeremy Corbyn, your mother went into labour. At eight o'clock we were taken into a room and knew then that we would not come out of it until we had you in your arms. All being well.

Yours was not a long, drawn-out affair.

I just know that at 10.32 pm on Friday August 21st 2015 I looked up and saw you hovering in the air, and this is what I thought to myself: *I have travelled all over this world. I have seen many things. I have sat on the steps of pyramids in Egypt and Mexico. I have crossed the bay of Naples with the sky above me filled with stars, having watched Maradona in his pomp. I have stood on hilltops in Japan and I have walked beaches in Brazil. I have walked through deep forests in America and stood in front of deep, magnificent oceans. I have known such beauty as to be convinced that Heaven is indeed upon earth.*

But I have never seen a more beautiful sight than that of you suspended above your mother.

Never.

The nurse took you to a corner and beckoned me over.

She asked me, 'Will you cut your son's cord?'

I thought straight away, 'This is one of the most beautiful jobs I have ever been given.' I was honoured to perform such a service for you, Rafi, so deeply honoured.

And then it was done, and you were screaming and that sound said, your life and your soul are now changed forever.

People came to me then and they told me that through you I would be able to experience a second childhood, one that would obliterate the deep unhappiness of my first. To be honest, I did not understand their reasoning. But now I see and feel the truth in their words.

Until you came along, a happy childhood to me was an abstraction. Unknowable. Invisible. I had no idea what it felt like. But now I do. I know because I look at you and I see it right there in front of me. I see it in your wide smile and hear it in your laughter. I feel it. You make it real to me. And because you do that it can now become a part of me. Just by living Rafi, you give me a joy and a beauty that robs the past of its darkness, gives me a peace and contentment previously denied me.

In past times, I had sought relief through many other avenues - music, films, books and football.

But you bring a much deeper experience and thus change, beautiful beautiful change, occurs inside of me. You make me embrace a totally new idea of myself.

Thank you, Rafi.

Ah – your name. At the moment you do not know this but it is Muslim in origin, means The Exalted One. One of your beautiful souled aunts gave it to us and I thought, well if Man U have The Special One, Spurs, the team you will play for, can have you, The Exalted One.

So Rafi it was although in truth you very nearly carried a completely different name.

At first - and I was deadly serious about this - I wanted your primary name to be *De Niro*. For a start, I think it a beautiful name. I truly do.

Yet behind that is the fact that I really wanted to honour the man whose work has had such impact upon me.

It was in De Niro's films - in particular Godfather 2, Raging Bull, Mean Streets, Taxi Driver and New York New York - that I learnt a valuable lesson - that it was okay to be me, to be a loner, okay to be someone who found conversation difficult, okay to be shy, inward-looking, awkward, a man with a fractured soul. In watching his films, De Niro gave me deep solace and a sense of identity.

De Niro was at that time mysterious, elusive. He was a dark horse, rarely spoke in public. His art was his communication. I tried to follow that path. But it wasn't mine to walk upon. It was his. I had to forge my own way. But in taking that journey I was given so much.

I understand that you - and others - may find it in some way disconcerting that I should look to a well-known Hollywood star for direction and instruction, that I should place such emphasis on his shoulders. But I needed to, Rafi, in fact *had* to, for I had no-one to guide me, no one at all.

I had arrived in London without family, without friends, without money. I was adrift and needed guidance so badly. It was De Niro who, through his craft, supplied it, seriously helped me in my time of need.

Of course, there were others whose friendship brought me knowledge and light but De Niro rose above them all. From De Niro, I learnt the real value of discipline. I have held myself to such demands ever since. You can see the proof on the book shelves in our sitting room. Over twenty books bear my name.

When I landed my first job as a staff writer at Melody Maker I did not take a holiday for the first two years. I just kept working. I think in ten years of writing for both Melody Maker and NME, I missed one deadline. I spent ten years writing millions of words for the music press

Of course, those who know me well might point out that such consistency was of no hardship to me. It was not as if I worked at a job I despised. I loved writing. It caused me pain and anguish but I loved it, especially the process of it. Why?

Because when I am writing I am in the moment. Everything in my life that is of a problematic nature disappears. Money, relationships, dissatisfaction with me, gone, vanished. All that matters is the now, and the piece I am writing. I had been given the magic that took away my thinking and replaced it with creation.

De Niro taught me to honour my craft, to place it first, to always seek to become better, whatever it takes. De Niro's films also gave me a sense of identity. They spoke to the Italian inside of me. Up to that point, I had nothing to define myself by. I had no class or its culture to shape me. Where do you place the orphan in the class system? Not being able to find an answer to that question created a damaging and hurting space inside of me.

Mean Streets, Raging Bull, and other great Italian American works, started to fix that painful gash. Those films then gave me dreams. Soon, I yearned to be as well dressed as Johnny Boy and as religious as Charlie.

I imagined myself sat round large wooden tables, wearing braces over a white vest, stabbing my fork into bowls of pasta, and expressing my feelings without fear of condemnation.

I wanted to stand up for myself and make points by gesticulating in true Neapolitan style. I wanted to be as inward as De Niro and a clever as Pacino in the Godfather films.

But I was too shy, too weak.

I was also too open to other influences. I kept shifting the scenery on set. One minute I would be playing my Italian card, the next minute I would be the fiery working class writer from the special Surrey town.

I became you, I became him, and I became them. I became everyone but myself.

But there was something else at work here Rafi and it was to do with my admiration for De Niro and his methods. I wanted to be as dedicated as he was to his art. I aspired to his intensity. I wanted to be as impressive in my field as he in his. Why? Because by setting my bar so high I was setting myself up to fail, which then allowed me to indulge myself in my aforementioned bad habit - that of fierce self-criticism born of self-destructive tendencies.

For example, when I discovered De Niro had learnt Sicilian for his role as the young Corleone in Godfather II, I determined myself to master the Italian language in the same time. I failed.

See, you said you were going to master Italian, but you didn't, and so they are right and so are you - you are worthless, without talent, without skill. Only a matter of time before the rest of the world cottons onto your essential worthlessness. In fact, they are already laughing at you behind your back at this very moment.

(In truth, I later discovered, De Niro only learnt the words needed for his role.)

No wonder De Niro in Raging Bull resonated so strongly with me. In that film, stricken with guilt over his actions, he allows other boxers to brutally punish him in the ring. Maybe that is exactly what I was doing, setting myself up all the time to take the punches because *that is all I knew*

I had a friend once who was horrified to see television footage of men whipping themselves in public as an act of religious devotion. He had a strong sense of who he was, and could not understand why anyone would want to hurt themselves in such manner.

But I did. I got it. For I did it. Every day.

Naturally, my strict Catholic upbringing - an altar boy at five - had its part to play in all this. I had been raised in a religion that told me that no matter how good I was, how devoted, how sincere, how generous to the poor and to the needy, I had been born in sin and thus would die and go to Hell a sinner. For me, there was no hope. Perfect for those who hate themselves.

Even so, I loved my religion. As a child I truly felt that we Catholics were superior to other religions. Other religions allowed their vicars to marry. Our priests were, ahem, pure... Our churches were beautiful and our Masses, conducted then in Latin, were mysterious, only for the chosen few.

I thought that way as a child, but as a teenager I left the church. I made up some excuse about a drunk being ejected from Midnight Mass one Xmas. In reality, it was because I now had music pushing me towards rebellion and thus I saw the Church in the same way I viewed the police or any other authority.

I have since returned to the fold, and am glad to discover new ways of thinking in action.

But it wasn't Catholicism alone that led me to such self-harm. It was the darkness of my childhood that forged my wayward thinking. Pure and simple

I adopted a stance of defiance. I was like De Niro in The Deer Hunter when he holds a bullet up and he says, 'this is this.' Which is how I operated. This is good, this is bad. You think otherwise then you are a fool and not worthy of my conversation. I think it is called arrogance and attention-seeking.

Writing this now I find it weird that two opposing and strong elements should be at work. I was shy but opinionated, extrovert but withdrawn. But I am also human, full of complexes and contradictions. Just like you, and everyone else walking this planet.

Which is why people like to put you in a box. Makes life so much simpler.

Back to Robert De Niro we must now go, and the name Rafi. Soon as I heard it, I knew De Niro was no longer viable as your moniker. My Bobby was out. You had your name. My heart told me that, Rafi.

What then worried me was that you did not have your full family history.

To know why, Rafi, reach to the book shelves and pull down two books of mine – The Looked After Kid and But We All Shine On - The Remarkable Orphans Of Burbank Children's Home.

The story of your father resides in those pages.

For I was born in a thunderstorm Rafi but know not the source of my lightning. How is such a thing possible? How can a man know his mother, yet still be deprived of his father's identity? *Non possible,* right?

Well, that is what they thought of my mother. In 1952 they put her inside a hospital and filled her with drugs. In 1957, she lay with someone.

In 1958 when her stomach had grown to a size that the authorities could no longer put down to their belief that she was Italian and prone to putting on weight, they asked her for the father's identity.

She refused to give it. Defiance, Rafi, sheer defiance (I carry that instinct of hers and it has both blessed and cursed me.).

She would not give up his name. I think I know why. I think she wanted something for herself, something that was hers and hers alone, something the hospital could never be a part of however much they tried.

They controlled every aspect of her life, Rafi.

But this they did not have in their grasp, and this she would not give unto them, whatever the consequences. Her secret would be hers for all time. Her defiance raged against the machine. And won. Unknown is the word written under the 'Father' section of my birth certificate.

The only problem with her recalcitrance is that when, fifteen years after my birth, I came to her and asked for his identity, she could not supply it. All her scrambled brain could give me was a name - Cruise. Or Cruz. That was it. No description and, more importantly, no knowledge of his nationality.

I tried to go back in time and find him. The records for your grandmother's hospital are kept - strangely enough - at a library in Woking, Surrey, about half a mile from my children's home. I went there one Saturday. It was my birthday.

Not sure which one, because when you get to my stage in life such events are not of importance. But I did reason it was precisely the sort of day that God would deliver unto me that which had to be known. Bit of advice, Rafi, never try and second-guess God.

I was given two bulky volumes that recorded the hospital's many activities, specifically meetings where patients were discussed. That is where I began my search.

Nothing. The nearest I came to a name beginning with C was a Crother or some such. Hours I spent meticulously running my finger down every page looking for that elusive name. Nothing was yielded unto me. So then I looked for staff names. Of course, I reasoned, given my so very deep intellect, he must have been a doctor.

Again, nothing. Mr Cruise or Mr Cruz was a ghost. On the train home I wondered about my mother. Had she given me his proper name? Maybe she had invented it at the time, not even knowing his real name. Maybe she had been... No, let's not go there.

But that is why, Rafi, one quarter of your blood remains unclaimed by country. I am sorry for that. Truly sorry. It pains me that you may not know the full nature of your blood.

So there is another path I am going to try. A DNA test. I have sent off for the equipment. Did it yesterday. Should be here any day now.

I give them saliva and then send it back to them. They return with the nationalities that are contained within my sample. I am betting the word 'Ireland' will be prominent. It is a feeling I have had for a long time, a small conviction that others have helped shape.

For example. We were out in one of your favourite parks in the summer, and do you remember that woman we got talking to who was Irish and married to a man from India? Well, the first thing she said to me was, 'You're Irish right? I'm from Ireland myself and as soon as I saw you I thought: *There is an Irish man.*'

Others have told me that my eyes are direct from County Cork. Maybe so, maybe not, all I know is that the mystery of my father's identity cannot continue for your sake. This is important, Rafi. You are human and roots are therefore crucial to your psyche. You need a sense of belonging, an identity of sorts.

I have come to know this as age has taken me over. My roots may be shattered but there are still many potent strands that serve me so well. There are roots in Italy.

There I have cousins and aunts. You are part of them, Rafi. There are roots in Yeovil. Two half-sisters and their children, and then their children. And now there is you.

Sounds kind of crazy, but I did not really understand such things nor indeed how deep the link runs between child and parent - until you arrived.

I heard people say they would die for their children and my head understood but not my heart. I met fathers who had given up their jobs to raise their children and my head understood but not my heart. You changed that, Rafi.

Now I say and do both those things. And I do so with love and conviction and joy. Because you are a delight, a national treasure that the country has not met yet. Writing so effusively reminds me of the times when I have been love-struck, lovesick, pining for that person until I ached. And when I was lucky enough to walk out with them I could not stop holding and kissing them.

It is exactly the same with you. I am forever hugging you and placing kisses on your cheeks, placing my lips on your forehead, your nose. Even when we go out walking I can't resist stopping the pram, tilting you back towards me and rubbing your head with mine. And the great thing about this is that this love will never fade. It will only increase. There is so much to love about you, so much you do which brings me true delight. And so much more to unfold. Now I want to live forever to witness it all.

You have these sounds you make which are new and fresh to my ears. When you see an aeroplane or a cat you shout out 'Ah! Ah!' There are others sounds as well. *Eh! Eh! De! De! Meh- Meh. Ber! Ber! Ba. Mhyrr...*

The one I love the most is when you are staring at something with great intensity and a whoop of delight suddenly emanates from your body. I love that sound.

It makes me sad that one day that sound will be gone, replaced by words, and I will never hear you talk like that again.

Then again, I can't wait for you to know language, to speak. Chats. Conversations. Precious communication. I want to get deep with you and silly with you. I want to enlighten if I can and then stay silent when it is best.

Maybe that is why I am writing these words right now at this point in your life, because at this very moment it is my only way of truly talking to you.

You have also caused me great anguish, none more so than that time in the doctor's office when you were given your third set of injections and your mother held you firm in her arms and you looked directly at me and yelped in such agony, a terrible sound, but worse were your eyes which screamed at me for help, any kind of help, eyes that said to me, *How can you let them cause me such pain and not do anything, how can you do that?* And I could not answer, all I could do was try and soothe you as best as I could, trying to deal with the knowledge that it wasn't the pain that hurt you so hard, it was the shock of your father's inaction.

And yes, I cried inside, cried a million tears for you in that moment.

I talk to you right now as a father although I have only ever known *father figures*. This caused me much worry where you are concerned. How, I kept asking myself, can I be a father to this child when I have no experience of fathers and the roles they play? How can I be something I have never experienced?

The first father I ever met was a man named Bill. He was married to the unbalanced woman who raised me from the age of four to ten. He was as helpless to her rage as I was. She snapped, he cowed. She roared, he ran.

When she asked him to fetch the wooden cane from the shed with which to beat my seven year-old body, he did so. Reluctance was heavy in his heart, I could see that - but he still he fetched and carried that which would beat and hurt me.

At a very early age, I stopped looking to him for salvation from her anger, her bitterness. I did not know it then but looking back but I see I did so because I had lost all respect for him. Even so, his life was tinged with sadness, for he was weak and could not overcome this defect. And that knowledge ruined him. He died at an early age.

The second father figure was the man who ran my children's home. But he too was unbalanced, obsessed with sex and alcohol. In later life, I would meet two girls from Burbank who claimed abuse against him. And their stories rang true.

Others at the home liked him but I never warmed to him. I left Burbank and met the best father figure - Geoff Garland. I lived in his house for a year or so after leaving Burbank. I had been invited there by my close friend, Geoff's son, Pete.

I was a nightmare. Did not know it at the time, but I see it now. Clearly.

Raised in a Home, I was used to a different way of living. I played my records loud. I walked their house in muddy shoes. I lived with no notification to them of my movements. I had little respect for their belongings.

In a children's home everything is on loan. Nothing belongs to you. Your surroundings belong to others. You have little respect for them. A chair is broken? Someone will bring in another. And this you carry onto adult life.

Geoff - and his wife, Mrs G - never said a word about my tardiness, my unruliness, my sheer carelessness. All they did was show me love and compassion.

If ever I think of a father I would like to have experienced, Geoff Garland comes to mind. He was a man of humour and a man of principle, a man worth studying.

But I only knew him a year, and then I was in London. He passed some years later and still I think of his warmth, his essential goodness, wrought in sturdy principles. And if I even need to experience them again, I just pick up the phone and call his son.

I met good men in London, Rafi, very good men. You know a few of them. Interestingly, some of them had been bestowed with fathers who loved them but were in many ways distant from them. English, in their ways.

I recall being in Sorrento and talking with a man who ran a hotel. 'Tell me something,' he said, 'I really like the English. They come to my hotel and are polite and cheerful and never a problem. I speak too many of them, and I like them, but one thing I do not understand – why on earth do they try and get rid of their children from their home as soon as possible? I don't understand. I love my children and I want to be with them all the time.'

My friends had fathers raised in a generation where emotion was not recognised. But any residue seems not to have over spilt into their children. In fact, they are all, to a man, great fathers. They care so deeply, loving above all.

And thus I looked to them and I asked them all a question. I said, 'I am worried. How do I become that which I have never known?'

And my great friend, Pete Barrett said this to me. 'My father was great, Paolo, a wonderful man but when my first daughter came along I felt exactly like you do right now. There is no secret to this just one rule - be there for him. That's all you can do. Be there. And the rest comes to you.'

Pete is one of my oldest friends, lives now in Australia (coincidentally, he, Russ and Pete Garland are all born on the same day) and his words were of such great value, Rafi, for they helped shape my new ambition. Because all I want now, Rafi, all I desire, is to be the best father and the best writer I can possibly be, and in that order.

Which means this: every time you turn round I will be standing there, my arms open. Up to you if they are needed or not. Just as long as I am there.

Talk of fathers brings mothers into view and - Actually Rafi, before we go any further, I have an idea - let's take a breather, get some fresh air, and go walking.

Let's strap you into your pram and then ease you out of the door and into a light wind that will caress your lips and eyes, and a sun that will intoxicate. Let us move towards the small park at the end of the road and chase the pigeons.

There! There!

Let me now put you on the swing, and ask you as I always do – 'Do you want to go higher than the sun?' And you will nod your head. 'Higher than the sky?' Again, a nod. 'Higher than the moon?' and then I will draw you back and push you forever upwards.

And after this, we will kick a ball and you will run for it with glee in your heart, your legs so strong yet so vulnerable still. You kick the ball into the road just as a bus passes.

You do make me laugh when we travel by bus. You flirt like crazy. You look around the passengers until you see the perfect prey, always a woman. You then fix that woman with your smile, and then, when she smiles back, you quickly turn your head in that shy manner of yours, and in doing so you have placed her in the palm of your hand - if only I had known such tricks in my youth.

On women, by the way, I offer no advice, Rafi. None at all. I can only give you this story.

Many years ago I lived near a wonderful road entitled the Stroud Green Road. To me, this road was the best of London. At the start of it was an Italian pizza joint which then led you to food outlets run by Poles, Argentinians, Mauritians, Mexicans, Rumanians, more Italians. Other shops were run by Asians and Europeans, all side-by-side, and no trouble.

One of my favourite places was Il Pappagone, a pizza joint run by two men both named Marco. One of the Marcos I'd met years back when I had written an article on Italians in London and interviewed his parents.

One day, about eleven o clock, I was walking down to the supermarket when he spotted me. He called me over.

'Hey Paolo, you write books, right?

'Sure do, Marco.'

'I want to write a book.'

I took a step back.

'Why? You run a very successful pizza joint. Why you would you want to put yourself through the agony? If you're serious, you have to wake up with the book on your mind, think and write about it all day, and then go to sleep with the damm thing on your mind?'

'Don't care. I want to write a book. Guess what I want to call it?'

'Go on.'

'I want to call it: *Women - What The Hell Do You Want?*'

Rafi, I have to tell you that is a question that has been asked since the start of the world - and is yet to be fully answered.

And that is all you need to know about the fairer sex, son, and may God bless you and keep you in your adventures. Past the bus stop we go to the shop where the woman is always delighted to see you, and always gives you a small toy which you carelessly toss away a minute later on Wood Green High Street, a street full of life and off beat colour and discordant noise, where the howl of the forgotten blends with the laughter of the young, where the cry of the drunkard meets the cry of the baby, a street where danger and beauty are bedfellows, a forgotten street, a street like so many, full of Savers, and Poundlands, and betting shops, Primark and a hundred-thousand charity shops, not a street for gentrification. Or, indeed, psycho-geography.

I am glad you are a London boy. I love this city, its people, the way it still keeps revealing itself to me. I have been here over 30 years now, and I still consider myself a stranger to it. I like that feeling. You won't have that, Rafi. You are not an outsider like I am.

This is your town full of splendour and magical characters, and you will know all its contours because they belong to you. That I like this street in Wood Green that we traverse is much to do with my perception of myself as working-class. Yet I am an orphan who attended Public School. Twice.

Still trying to figure that one out? So am I.

But class is another illusion, Rafi, another one to avoid. I used to define myself by it. Especially in my music-press days. I styled myself as the bolshy working-class writer, full of venom for others, ready to fight anyone in my way. Just like Johnny Boy in Mean Streets.

I remember being at the Limelight Club near Soho and getting convinced the singer Mick Hucknall was laughing at me. So I went over and asked him what he found so hilarious. As he began to give his answer I studied his arms and fists and realised my chances of success in a scrap with him were worse than nil.

Luckily, my very good friend Mr Halfon, dragged me away before anything could develop. I now say to Michael, a long-term resident and lover of Italia, *Sono molto dispiaciuto per il mio comportamento*. Me angry young man back then. Me angry working class man back then.

But my class was just another title, Rafi, another category, another illusion, another misplaced identity.

Avoid such traps. Just know thyself and bring forth your spirit, Rafi, for that spirit never ages; it is strong, endurable. More than that, it is the very essence of you. It is what you will use to achieve your dreams if you are lucky enough to be given them. It is also the voice that remonstrates with you when you go against its grain.

Onwards we go up the High Street. People sit against dirty walls and beg. One homeless guy has a bollard next to him. He grabs it and sings into it, 'Welcome to the Hotel California, such a lovely place….' And I can't help but smile.

I always give the homeless money. I have to. My spirit insists upon it. 60 per cent of the homeless were once in care like I was, Rafi. I have a duty to them. So do you and there for the grace of God go I.

Into the library we go and straight to the film section. I find nothing to excite me and that worries me a bit. Recently, a friend of mine visited his father, now in his nineties.

'Want to watch a film?' he asked him. 'No,' he replied, 'I feel like I have seen them all now.'

I don't feel that way but I *know* what he meant. Which worries me.

I can sense your impatience so I head for the exit and back out into the street and through the people, all kinds of people, all kinds of faces, some strong, determined, others belligerent at my enquiry into them, some shy, some beautiful, some to excite the blood, others with menace defined in their eyes, all swallowed up in their lives and cares and desires and ambitions, some moving fast, some moving carefully, many smoking, many dressed in dark colours and unremarkable clothing, some shopping, but always energy and action here, all fighting something invisible, and there goes the police siren again, the true soundtrack to Wood Green's activity, and we know this because no-one takes any note of its urgent sound for they are as used to it as they are breathing.

The police siren – that's the sound of Wood Green.

And as we walk I think of how much enjoyment our journeys together bring me. There are many reasons, primarily to do with the time spent with you. But there are other bonuses. For it is on these excursions that I am able to create ideas, to think about work, to think specifically about this piece of writing.

For example, just now as we walked down the High Street, came a major realisation. You recall earlier when I was telling how you had opened me up, made me so vulnerable that tears of mine were often falling but that I could not find the source of their being? I think I have it Rafi.

I think it's because that all being well, all being good, all being as it should be, at some point, my beautiful and cherished son, I will have to leave you on this earth and venture elsewhere. The thought of you not by my side, that's where my sorrow is located, in the inevitable parting brought on by time's passing.

Fact remains, as I remarked in another work of mine, I now have more years beyond me than in front and although I am certain we have many years to experience each other in, there will come the day of my passing to another place, another home and you will not be able to follow.

But I know this also Rafi, you will shine out and that light will somehow reach me and all will be as it should be.

At the park we chase some pigeons again but the wind drops cold and so I rush you home and there on the mat, a small package. I open it as you squirm like a crazed fish, turning this way and that, so anxious to leave the pram and look Rafi – the DNA kit has arrived.

After settling you on the sofa with your milk, I open the box. Inside a tube, a lid, a plastic bag and a self-addressed box. In the lid is fluid. The instructions are simple. Fill the tube with saliva, put on lid and let fluid from the lid into the saliva by turning.

I follow the instructions. Never used to. Always baulked at suggestions. Now, as I grow older I tend to accept and listen. Unless it is the current Government talking…………

And then I come into the room, remove the milk bottle from your grasp, and tell you I have bad news.

I must bid you farewell.

Ciao Ciao Rafi –Ciao.

For to Italy I must now go. I do not want you to leave you but I am bound for Sorrento, Rafi, to gain some much needed perspective on this work, to gather up more ideas, more words, and experience my first ever Italian Xmas.

Let me tell you what will happen.

Close your eyes. Both of them. That's it. Now think of this.

First, I will rise early and board an early morning plane. I will arrive in the sunshine of Naples reminiscent of loving spring days, and take a bus to the place of your grandmother's birth, and from there to the house of my Zia Gilda, the woman who married your uncle, Gigorne, and God rest his soul.

In their small kitchen Gilda will bake a pie and I will tell her how happy I am to see her. Hers will be a small smile, which lets me know she feels exactly the same. There is a deep connection between myself and Gilda, Rafi.

When your auntie Nina visited last year, Gilda told her that when she met me for the first time she knew no English whatsoever and I had no Italian. Yet it did not matter. She understood my words through body language alone.

Love is here, Rafi, love given to me by such warm people, such loving people, such *funny* people. That love, given without any attention to it, will allow me to rest and find balance. That love will soothe and calm me.

In Sorrento with my family I learn to let go of all and simply be.

On Xmas night, I will go to the theatre and watch a play in Italian; the next night I will attend a wonderful gospel concert in the Cathedral. I will play Italian card games and watch Italian TV. I will visit many churches and pray for you Rafi and in doing so see your face in lighted candles which I hope will burn forever.

And then I will return to Zia Gilda and I will play with her grandchildren and laugh with my cousins. I will walk to the harbour and breathe in deep the Neapolitan air.

I will traverse the town's streets, those ancient cobbled streets and let history soak into my bones, and I will sit in cafes and I will think about this work and in doing so I will come to a decision, a major decision.

It is time to write about my past - and then let it go. The time has come to take my burden, place it upon paper for the last time and then put it upon the eagle's wings and let it soar into the sky.

It is time to liberate myself Rafi, time to move on from my past and its grave and stultifying presence and look to you with fresh eyes and soul.

I note here, by the way, Rafi that I have used the word soul many times in this piece. That was part of Sorrento as well, the realisation of the intent that has always lived behind my words, the ambitions I carry for them every time I put finger to keypad.

Since I began writing, I have never aimed at the head, the intellect. I am incapable of such a task.

Mine is simply an instinctive approach, driven and guided only by the osmosis of so many books, so many newspapers, so many magazines. Samuel and David, the two soul singing brothers used to talk about how they got what they got the hard way but now they are going to make better every day, and that reveals my writing purpose.

I am a soul man with a soul pen, seeking to move hearts – not minds. In reacting to music or films or books or any art in fact, all I wanted was to produce words that moved me in the same way that those works did, to try and reflect some of the emotions the best of it had engendered in me.

Deep theory always seemed to me a barren land; the soul in all things is what I wanted to reveal.

In doing so, some people applauded my honesty, my bravery in exposing my thoughts and feelings, especially in the case of my two books about Care.

And this process was heightened even further when people who had experienced care thanked me for my work. 'That book is me,' one care leaver told me about The Looked After Kid and I was so proud and so moved.

But now as I board the plane home I know now that this will be the last time I go into my past. I refuse to cling onto it. I refuse to define myself by it. I need to move upwards to the spheres with you Rafi and I can't do so with such baggage for it keeps me tied to the ground.

You can open your eyes now, Rafi. Look – I am home and so happy to see you.

I put down my suitcase and I hug you and kiss you and then lie beside you on the bed and bid you goodnight and tell you to head for the stars, Rafi, and take from the moon, for now as you drift into darkness I will tell all about my hurting past for the very last time.

Let me repeat – I was born in a thunderstorm and know not the source of my lightning. In 1957, my mother lay down with person unknown and gave herself unto him. And thus a seed was planted. On July 11th 1958, it flowered and I arrived on this earth.

After two days in my mother's arms, a nurse removed me from her love, her care, click clacked her way down a stone corridor, opened a door and threw me upwards into the immense blackness.

As I flew upwards from the nurse's arms, the wind of great misfortune picked me up and it took me high and then it took me low. I was thrown sideways and downwards.

I swooped upwards and then lost my balance and fell, and the blackness was never ending, surrounding me on all sides. The wind pushed me further downwards and then suddenly changed. I swirled in excelsis and flew the skies. Clouds were my resting place, the sea was a mattress until came the day when I was allowed to open my eyes and when I did, I saw that I had landed at the feet of a woman. I looked up. I looked into her face and – snap! – the deal was done and my fate secured.

Her face carried traces of anxiety, her eyes flickered a little bit too quickly. I took no note. I was four years old.

At first, she was firm but not unkindly. I detected a stern nature but not cruelty. She had patience. She sat and taught me to read. I ran with that discipline, showed great promise and this pleased her. For she had a plan.

Prestigious public school – Haileybury, no less - then onto Oxford, that is where I was headed, Rafi. I know hard to believe of me, hard to imagine the straw hat and the boat on the river and a posh voice on me.

Yet, despite her smile, I was aware, even then, that this world I had entered was slightly askew. Clues were placed in front of me. There was the room I was forbidden to enter. The husband who could not do as he pleased. The dog whose yapping frightened me so yet no one moved to calm my fears. The austere atmosphere created by the long silences at meal times. The lack of joy. The lack of faithfulness to *life.*

I am not at all sure when she first hit me. It would no doubt have been a slap but the physical hurt that allowed the expression of her unassuageable and deep anger, slowly progressed.

There were the nights Rafi, when, she bent me over the kitchen table and caned my seven year old body. There were days when from nowhere her hand would snap viciously slap my head, sometimes my cheeks, which she left burning.

There were days Rafi when she would kick me.

But this was the least of her weapons. Physical you can bear. It was her tongue that hurt deep and true, that caused me the greatest hurt, the greatest suffering, and left me with the wounds that you now heal.

'Look at you - you are so ugly.' 'How could God make a boy so stupid?' 'You really are such a worthless human being.' 'No one will ever like you.' 'Look in the mirror at yourself. Have you ever seen such a pathetic child?' 'Shut up Paul, I don't want to hear your voice.'

This day in and day out, my soul burnt by the sharp acid which sprang from her mouth and poured into my body where it melted all goodness and energy and confidence in myself. It did its' job. Brilliantly.

My suffering was ruled by her capricious nature, her unpredictable moods shifting at lightning pace, impossible to keep up with. One minute happy, one minute angry, one minute scathing, one minute light, one minute sad, one, minute aggressive, one minute understanding, one minute the terror of all terrors.

I was seven years old Rafi and in the face of this onslaught I became silent. I withdrew. I was helpless against the storm of her hatred and bitter unhappiness. There was just one period of relief.

Rafi, you know how last summer, I used to suddenly stop the pram and tilt you upwards and implore you to look at the beautiful deep blue sky and those mystical clouds, and take in this vast and immense beauty?

That is because the only relief I got from this woman occurred when she left on a six month work project in India. My two grandmothers came to look after me. The husband was also there. Suddenly, a magic was present. The rooms we sat in became light and airy. At the kitchen table there was talk and smiles. I felt a warmth in that house that I had never felt before. And because of it I played carefree in the garden. I smiled. I became a child. I threw off my shackles.

I ran and I did not trip. I climbed and I did not fall. I jumped and I landed without hurt.

It was summer and during that time of belonging to the world through love, I would go into the garden and lie down on sweet smelling grass and spend hours staring at the clouds moving across that wonderful sky in such a stately manner, and I would imagine myself upon one of those thick white clouds and I would see myself leaping from one to the next and I would dream of life without her and I would – and then she was home.

Need I say more, Rafi? Is there value in describing the increasing of her hatred towards me, the cupboard she now regularly locked me or the tying up of my hands at bedtime to discourage scratching, or the vicious scrubbing of my skin in a hotel shower because the Mediterranean sun had turned me brown? Need I say more, Rafi? Need I make clear her daily disillusionment with my progress and the suffering it brought me?

I think not. All you need know is that I retreated inside again. I became an outsider, pushed there by this woman's deep hatred of – herself. For no one who carries honourable self-esteem acts in such a fashion. If love is in the soul it is impossible to act in the way she did.

Where had she been denied this love? In her childhood, I later discovered. Her brilliant brother had taken the spotlight and she had been placed in the shadows. And in those shadows she plotted her revenge. I had no idea that I would be her first victim.

In case you are wondering where the world was during this period of such horror, this time in which my childhood was taken from me and then smashed into a thousand different pieces, two people tried to save me, Rafi

One was a social worker. In 1965, she smelt the fear in the house and urged for my removal. Her request was refused. And then she was removed from my case. My next social worker could not fathom her thinking, her opinions. He did not have the capacity or the imagination to understand why a child living in such a nice house should be placed elsewhere.

His report was titled, 'The Art Of Gracious Living' in which he explained why I would be staying with these wonderful people who were to give me such great opportunities in life.

I do love irony.

The second person was a teacher. Mr Frith. He combined two qualities I eagerly admired as a child. He taught Latin and played football. He was also astute and sensitive. He saw my fear in his classroom. He looked over at me and he knew I was too quiet, too inward, too distracted, too *still*.

He made enquiries. But he was not clever enough. His questions came to the attention of the woman who looked after me.

I was removed from his school within a week.

Oscar writes, 'Suffering is one very long moment.' Mine stretched over five and a half years, day in and day out. Like Oscar I was in a gaol but I had committed no crime. Dostoyevsky should be my touchstone not Oscar. But Oscar saw and knew what I came to see – that time never moves more slowly than when one suffers at the hands of others. Tick…..tick…..tick.

And then one day this woman removed me from her care. She click clacked down her hallway, opened the door and then threw me out into that which I knew so well – the immense darkness.

Again, God came to my help. He put my soul on ice. He did so to protect me from others. I was going into care. I needed some kind of defence. Which is why God froze my soul. I thanked him later on.

At my first children's home, I sat in a tree for two or three days. I ached for someone to come and take me in their arms and love all the hurt away. And they did come but as you will discover Rafi, what you yearn for is often given to you, just never in the way you expect.

John Brown - and God rest that kindly man's soul - reached out to me.

His wife Molly, who also ran the home, did so as well but John I connected with because John made me feel safe, made me feel special. From April of 1968 to August of that year, he began healing my deep deep wounds.

He was the kindly Uncle all children dream about.

He let me watch lunchtime cricket with him. He spoke softly to me. He never raised his voice He respected me. If I had no words for him that that was fine. He would just smoke his pipe and smile at me a lot.

He was everything an adult should be to a child and of course I was forced to leave him for the world is often unintentionally cruel and the home he ran a stop gap. No kids got to stay there permanently although I would have moved the heavens to do so.

If I could have stayed with John and Molly Brown, I would not have suffered half as much as I did. What that woman did to me in six years, their love would have put right in two. But it was not to be.

Burbank Children's Home in Woking Surrey is where I laid my head for the next eight years of my life. My life there exists in two books, Rafi and although just to write that sentence brings me such deep joy, I do not want to re-visit ground already documented.

All I know is that there is not one experience of care Rafi. All of us feel life in a children's home in such different ways. For some it is destruction, for some it is salvation.

For some it is a horror show. For some it is a breeze. For my part, I did not even know such places existed apart from in the pages of the book, Oliver Twist by Charles Dickens, a book I had devou- sorry, have just got an Email from the DNA people and it looks important..

Damm. They could not get a reading off the tube I sent them. How disappointing is that? I was so looking forward to discovering once and for all my true nationality and therefore yours.

On the plus side, they have sent me a second kit for me to use. I do so and we go back out and post it.

We return home and into the sitting room.

I look over at you. You stare at me with those great dark eyes, that face which is tilted always - I am so happy to say - towards anticipation of fun and pleasure.

Only yesterday you were the size of a twig and now look at you, Little Man, kicking that ball in the hallway and then chasing it, a smile writ large upon your tender face.

I see now that is how the healing works. For when you smile, Rafi, so do I. Laughter acts in the same way. You love it when I tickle your neck. The laugh that erupts out of you is so pure and so deep and so joyful that no music has been made to match it. There is nothing – nothing whatsoever - but pure absolute enjoyment in that sound.

And before you know it I am laughing in exactly the same manner with no edge or holding back, just you and I locked in a joy which means that all that is bad or unworthy is banished forever.

Smiles and laughter are precisely that which brings a boy sat alone in a tree back into the garden where the others play.

This is what you do Rafi and you don't even know you are doing it. Of course, I am getting conscious here that my words here paint you as this Boy Wonder, direct from the celestial sky.

You know of course that is not true. You have some terrible habits.

The way you rush into my room and demand to sit on my lap and hit the keys of my computer. This is when of course I am writing this book and concentrating as hard as I can.

Or that way you have of fighting me every step of the way as I try to dress you, of wriggling and turning and screaming, as I try to put on a top or a pair of jeans, and when finally everything is on and we are about to leave, you suddenly make it clear that your nappy now needs changing. So I have to undress you, wash you and then we start all over again.

Or yesterday, when I spent half an hour preparing your lunch, then sat you at the table, put the food in front of you, went into the kitchen to get you a drink and when I returned, you had tipped the whole meal onto the floor.

I stared at the mess and was just about to say something, and then you smile. You smiled that smile Rafi, the one that says 'kind of funny isn't it?'

And you are right. It is. Funny.

Let me tell you my beautiful boy you are going to go an awful long way with that smile for it will spark up that which is good in others. And they in turn will give that back to you.

As I look at your smile and drink in its dreamlike quality, the thought of care suddenly takes centre stage in my mind. It moves and dances towards me and then it stops and demands some kind of definition. I reach for adjectives – scary, turbulent, liberating - but am quickly made aware that there are better ways to meets its demands.

For me Rafi there are two types of care – there is the care stored in my teenage memory bank, the memories of Burbank and all its people, the history that we created together which will be with all of us forever and forever, amen.

And then there is the care which is like a friend who has no shelter and he comes and asks you if he can stay with you for he has nowhere to go and, of course, you say yes and you let him into your house, and you give him a room and he lives there for months on end until one day he packs his bags, and then he leaves without even a thank you or a gift or a card of gratitude.

And you sit down and you think what a mean spirited and bitter man. And you think that way for many months until one day you go up into your loft to retrieve an idea, and you find on the shelf that he has left you a series of thank you gifts, all laid out for you. And that is how care was for me - it gave me qualities that only in later life were revealed to me.

Courage was one of Care's many gifts to me. These words could not have been written without such a quality. I reveal myself to you Rafi for you are my son and it feels right to do so, it honours our relationship, elevates it to where it should be.

These words of mine may mean nothing whatsoever to you but that is not the point. Care gave me the bravery to write them so that you could discover and know in full the love that runs behind every sentence I write to you.

Care turns its charges into either saints or sinners - and often into both. And thus it was for me. The dark places it took me too in my mind have no place here but the compassion it poured into my soul needs recognition.

I have now come to understand that in Care I was given that which I thought had been denied me – a family.

All of us at Burbank – especially Jimmy and Colin and Des and Martin but also Norman, Esther, Fred, David, Stephen, Andrew, and so many others, were bonded together in our experiences to the degree that families operate from. As I write this I see their faces shining before me and I bless each and every one. For they are my bedrock, just as much as those I have been lucky enough to know in later years, have been my sturdy pillars.

Many people have come to my side at varying stages in my life. Some have stayed. Others have fallen away. But they have all acted with such goodness that one can only form the conviction that most human beings are essentially decent souls.

I can think this way because Care taught me to be non-judgemental. Whoever landed at Burbank was one of us. Did not matter where his or her lightning had struck, or in what part of the world the wind of misfortune had carried him from. Did not matter. They were in Care. They were an equal. I have taken this into later life.

Without Care I do not believe I would have inhabited so many different worlds. Without Care I would not have had the strength to move forward. For better or worse, Care shaped me Rafi and I thank Care for that.

As for the woman who placed me in its grasp, I have to forgive her. It is imperative I do so for only by that action can I rise above. From my heart, I pluck out all my anger and resentment and bitterness and I forgive her just as I forgive all those who have hurt me in the past.

This is not as many might see it, a weakness. It is about freedom. Feelings and emotions, both light and dark, bind us to others. When they are mired in beauty and love it is a wonderful thing. From it comes sustenance and wisdom and a deep happiness. But if they are mired in anger or revenge then they are ugly and damaging.

The point is that whether it be love or hate we are still connected and that connection either liberates, in the case of love, or it keeps us in jail, as in the case of hate.

Therefore, I have forgiven all who have sought to hurt me. I have also in later years, set out to ask forgiveness for those I know I have wronged.

Again, this is seen as weakness but I tell you now, it takes great strength to go down on ones knees and say with all your heart - *Sono molto dispiaciuto per il mio comportament.*

It was the brave sprit of Care and the push of God that found me the courage to do so.

There are those who refused my words of penitence and those who hugged me back. Again, it is the action not the result that is of importance.

Jesus warned his people do not go to the altar unless you have made right with your brothers and sisters and this I have sought to do. I have done so that I may shake loose of all and look with you towards the new horizons that you have opened up so gloriously before me.

I suggest therefore that we take the following action.

This destructive past of mine? Let's destroy it. Once for all. Let's gather it up and place it in a sack.

Let's take that sack to the top of the hill where the Palace stands and open it and throw it back to the wind on which it came.

Or let's open the sack and spill those dark memories onto the ground and crush them joyfully with our feet. Grind them into the earth where they belong. Stamp on them like you do when you meet deep puddles in the street and so delight in them that you splash the dark water until all is no longer visible and can live no longer.

Or we can shape them into a football and kick them back into that immense darkness that I will never return to now that you are here by my side. I'll be Maradona. You be Dele Alli. Over to you, son.

And then in the fading sunset, let us walk, hand in hand, father and son, love upon love.

And at some point let's both stop and turn our heads upwards to the black sky, and then I will say, 'Look Rafi,' and you will look up, and I will point to the small glowing light in the sky and I will sing, *Twinkle twinkle little star, how I wonder how you are, up above the world so high, like a diamond in the sky......*

And you, my darling young son, will look up at me - and you will smile.

Yours.

PS. Rafi look at what has just arrived. Finally. My DNA results.

And they are –

ITALY / GREECE – 35 %

EUROPE WEST – 22%

IRELAND 12%

GREAT BRITAIN 9%

IBERIAN PENINSULA 8%

EUROPEAN JEWISH 4%

SCANDINAVIA 3%

WEST ASIA 7%

Better consider packing our bags, Rafi. We maybe going on a trip pretty soon.